A Busy Day

By Brian Sargent

Consultants
Chalice Bennett
Elementary Specialist
Martin Luther King Jr. Laboratory School
Evanston, Illinois

Ari Ginsburg
Math Curriculum Specialist

Children's Press®
A Division of Scholastic Inc.
New York Toronto London Auckland Sydney
Mexico City New Delhi Hong Kong
Danbury, Connecticut

Designer: Herman Adler Design
Photo Researcher: Caroline Anderson
The photo on the cover shows a girl checking her watch during her busy day.

Library of Congress Cataloging-in-Publication Data

Sargent, Brian, 1969-
  A busy day / by Brian Sargent.
      p. cm. — (Rookie read-about math)
   ISBN 0-516-24964-9 (lib. bdg.)   0-516-29811-9 (pbk.)
  1. Time—Juvenile literature. 2. Day—Juvenile literature. I. Title.
II. Series.
  QB209.5.S27 2006
  529'.7—dc22
                                2005019969

CHILDREN'S PRESS, and ROOKIE READ-ABOUT®,
and associated logos are trademarks and/or registered trademarks
of Scholastic Library Publishing. SCHOLASTIC and associated logos
are trademarks and/or registered trademarks of Scholastic Inc.

3 4 5 6 7 8 9 10 R 15 14 13 12 11 10 09 08   62

It's Saturday. I have a lot to do. I hope I stay on time!

I wake up at 7:00.

I use my alarm clock to make sure I do not sleep too long.

6

I get dressed quickly.

It takes me about one
second to pull on a sock.

One second is about the time it takes to say "One, one thousand."

Many people can do a jumping jack in one second.

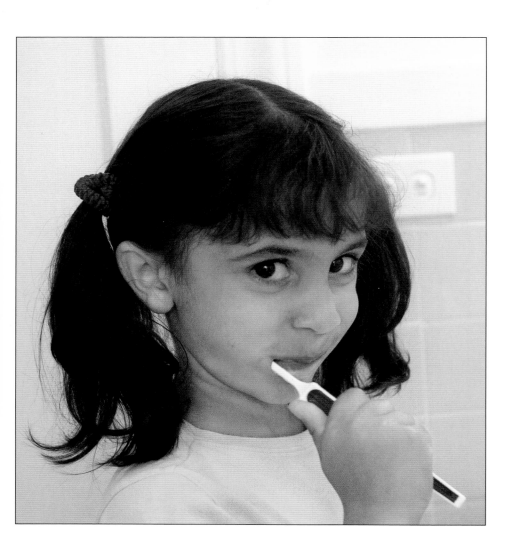

10

I brush my teeth.

It takes about one minute
to brush teeth.

One minute is sixty seconds long.

You can sing the Alphabet Song about three times in one minute.

13

14

Soccer practice is first.

It begins at 8:00. It lasts for one hour. That means it ends at 9:00.

An hour is sixty minutes long.

It takes about one hour to make and bake a cake.

18

After soccer practice I have a swimming lesson.

It takes thirty minutes to ride my bike to the swimming pool.

Thirty minutes is half of an hour.

My swimming lesson begins at 9:45. Another name for 9:45 is a quarter to ten.

At 10:30, my swimming lesson ends.

I need to dry off and change my clothes.

It's 11:00. Oh no! My friend's birthday party begins at 12:00 noon.

I need to hurry home and wrap her present.

Wrapping the present takes too long. I'm fifteen minutes late to the party!

It is 12:15. Another name for 12:15 is a quarter after twelve.

There are fun games at
the party.

My favorite is the race.

We won by three seconds!

Wow! Today has been a long day.

I have been busy for eight hours.

I'm happy to be back home!

29

Words You Know

alarm clock

bike

cake

present

race

sing

soccer practice

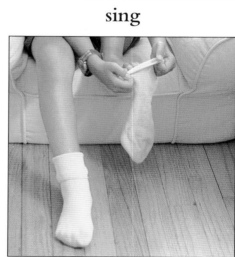

sock

31

Index

About the Author

Brian Sargent is a middle-school math teacher. He lives in Glen Ridge, New Jersey, with his wife Sharon and daughters Kathryn, Lila, and Victoria. He can brush his teeth in less than one minute.

Photo Credits